ENTERTAINMENT

DATE   PLACE   AMOUNT   REASON

ENTERTAINMENT

DATE   PLACE   AMOUNT   REASON

Times have changed. Self-published authors are on the rise, dominating a large percentage of the book market. Readers are discovering new authors every day. Authors are publishing new books every hour. It's a whirlwind of possibility as a self-published author.

However, the main con of having your own business is taxes. Not only are they stressful to think about, they require a large chunk of your time to organize (and we all know, time is money when you run your own business). Sure, you can get an accountant; many authors do. However, you still need to keep your records together and organized, or you'll have nothing to take to that accountant.

There are more pros than one could think of by being your own boss, but taxes simply isn't one of them.

This guide was designed to help keep your files, dates, and receipts all in one place. While this guide was created with self-published authors in mind, it truly can work for anyone with their own small business.

Please note, I am not an accountant. This guide is not meant to replace an accountant or represent the current tax laws (as they change yearly). It is merely a guide to make sure you get every deduction and keep every record possible.

ENTERTAINMENT

For authors, entertainment expenses can seem like a gray area at times. Generally speaking, a writer doesn't have clients and can't exactly write during a theater performance. However, there are a few situations that may apply to you.

One deduction that qualifies is meals as entertainment. For example, if you treat your editor to a meal while discussing how to move forward with your newest manuscript, the cost of the meal is considered entertainment and is deductible by 50%. This also is true for all individuals associated with your writing (eg: cover designer, agent, formatter, etc).

Another example would be a charitable benefit. Let's say you attend a charity ballet performance with your agent. The face value of the tickets would be deducible as entertainment.

If you think it would be considered entertainment, place it in this group. You can always move the deduction to another category should your accountant suggest it.

Note Be careful not to deduct twice. If you're deducting meals as entertainment, you cannot deduct them again under meals and travel.

ENTERTAINMENT

TAPE A 5" BY 7" MANILA ENVELOPE TO THIS PAGE TO KEEP YOUR RECEIPTS AND RECORDS FOR THIS CATEGORY ORGANIZED.

HOME OFFICE

ONE OF THE MOST OVERLOOKED TAX DEDUCTIONS AUTHORS CAN TAKE IS THE HOME OFFICE DEDUCTION. MANY TIMES THIS IS BECAUSE AUTHORS PICK UP THEIR LAPTOP AND WRITE WHENEVER THE INSPIRATION COMES. THEREFORE, THEY DON'T REALLY HAVE AN OFFICE. HOWEVER, IF YOU HAVE A SPACE THAT YOU DO MOST OF YOUR WRITING BUSINESS IN, THE SAVINGS YOU COULD GET IS WORTH THE WORK NEEDED TO TAKE THIS DEDUCTION.

HOME OFFICE DEDUCTIONS ARE BASED ON THE PERCENTAGE OF YOUR HOME YOU USE FOR YOUR BUSINESS. FOR EXAMPLE, LET'S SAY YOUR HOME IS 2,000 SQUARE FEET AND YOUR OFFICE IS 300 SQUARE FEET; YOU WOULD NEED TO DETERMINE WHAT PERCENTAGE OF YOUR HOME IS USED FOR BUSINESS. IN THIS CASE, BY DIVIDING THE SQUARE FOOTAGE OF THE OFFICE BY THE SQUARE FOOTAGE OF THE HOME (280 ÷ 1,800), WE DETERMINE THAT THE OFFICE IS 15.5% OF THE HOME. NOW THAT WE KNOW THE PERCENT, LET'S DISCUSS THE VARIOUS ITEMS THAT CAN BE DEDUCTED.

FIRST, THERE ARE DIRECT EXPENSES. DIRECT EXPENSES ARE THOSE INCURRED DIRECTLY FOR THE OFFICE SPACE. PAINTING THE WALLS, INSTALLING A NEW LIGHT FIXTURE, ETC. IF YOU DO REPAIRS THAT ARE ON THE ROOM IN QUESTION, THOSE ARE DIRECT EXPENSES AND THE TOTAL COST CAN BE DEDUCTED.

NEXT IS INDIRECT EXPENSES. THESE DEDUCTIONS ARE MORE COMMON AND WILL MOST LIKELY BRING YOU YOUR BIGGEST DEDUCTION. SINCE A PORTION OF YOUR HOME IS CONSIDERED BUSINESS PROPERTY, PART OF THE COST OF KEEPING UP YOUR HOME BECOMES BUSINESS WRITE-OFFS. SO IF YOUR OFFICE TAKES UP 15.5% OF YOUR HOME, YOU CAN CLAIM AND DEDUCTION 15.5% OF THE ELECTRIC AND WATER BILLS, GAS BILLS, HOMEOWNER'S INSURANCE, SECURITY FEES, REPAIRS AND MAINTENANCE, AND MORE.

YOUR TAX DEDUCTION SOFTWARE OR ACCOUNTANT WILL DO THE MATH FOR YOU, BUT IT IS IMPORTANT TO KEEP RECEIPTS AND STATEMENTS TO TAKE THIS DEDUCTION. WRITE DOWN EACH MONTHLY BILL AND STORE THE BILLS IN A SAFE PLACE SO YOU CAN PRESENT THEM COME TAX TIME.

Home Office

Provider	Amount	Direct/Indirect

HOME OFFICE

PROVIDER	AMOUNT	DIRECT/INDIRECT

Home Office

TAPE A 5" BY 7" MANILA ENVELOPE TO THIS PAGE TO KEEP YOUR RECEIPTS AND RECORDS FOR THIS CATEGORY ORGANIZED.

Marketing and Advertising

As a self-published author, there is a lot of work that goes into getting your books in front of readers. It takes a lot of time, and a great deal of marketing materials and advertising. In the traditional publishing world, this job would fall on the publisher and/or agent. However, as an indie, it requires you to do the work, but it also gives you more control.

When you attend book signings, you need swag like business cards, bookmarks, leaflets and more with your information for potential new readers. You need a website for them to discover your newest works.

Additionally, you need to broaden your fan base. Reach readers all over the world by advertising on social media, book blogs, along with Amazon and other book retailers.

All these costs are actual an investment in the future of your business. Start small, and gradually go larger with your marketing and advertising. A bonus is, you get to deduct the costs from your taxes at the end of the year. Even the cost of your website is deductible; so be sure to keep track of all you invest in getting your name out there!

Marketing and Advertising

Date	Payment to	Amount	Reason

Marketing and Advertising

Date	Payment to	Amount	Reason

Marketing and Advertising

DATE	PAYMENT TO	AMOUNT	REASON

Marketing and Advertising

DATE	PAYMENT TO	AMOUNT	REASON

Marketing and Advertising

TAPE A 5" BY 7" MANILA ENVELOPE TO THIS PAGE TO KEEP YOUR RECEIPTS AND RECORDS FOR THIS CATEGORY ORGANIZED.

MEALS

Writing off the cost of food and drink while traveling is something many authors tend to forget. It's so easy to toss the receipts or forget about them completely.

Meals are deductible by 50 percent of the purchase price. This includes the entire cost of the bill (food/drink, sales tax, and gratuity). If you're not deducting them, that's money you're throwing away when it comes to your taxes.

Regarding meal costs while traveling, authors can only take this deduction if they are honestly out of town (eg: grabbing a White Chocolate Mocha at your favorite coffee joint before heading home to write is not deductible). To qualify as travel, the period of time away from home must require you rest or sleep during the trip. So unless it's unusually long, meals during a day trip are not deductible.

Additionally, if you decide to bring your family along for the trip, only your meals are deductible. The meals for your children and/or spouse would be considered personal, not business. To avoid confusion, it is best to pay two separate bills, or get an itemized bill so you can deduct the cost of only your meal.

Be careful and keep good records when taking a meal deduction. The IRS rules on this particular deduction can be somewhat complicated. It is best to keep good records and bring them to your accountant so they can calculate this deduction for you.

Note Meeting for lunch with your editor, graphic designer, or other professionals tied to your books is deductible, given you spend time before during or after the meal talking in depth about work. However, this would fall under entertainment, not meals.

MEALS

DATE	RESTAURANT	AMOUNT	REASON

MEALS

DATE	RESTAURANT	AMOUNT	REASON

MEALS

DATE	RESTAURANT	AMOUNT	REASON

MEALS

DATE RESTAURANT   AMOUNT   REASON

Meals

TAPE A 5" BY 7" MANILA ENVELOPE TO THIS PAGE TO KEEP YOUR RECEIPTS AND RECORDS FOR THIS CATEGORY ORGANIZED.

Miscellaneous Expenses

When dealing with the world of taxes, it is hard to know what category certain dedications might fall in to. Perhaps you're not sure if your meal qualifies as a deduction. Maybe you purchased something for both business and personal purposes.

This section is for business expenses you incur that you're not quite certain qualify or aren't sure what category to put them in.

This way, you do not lose track of the expense and can bring it to the attention of your accountant or tax attorney. It can always be removed if it doesn't qualify, but you certainly don't want to miss out on a valuable deduction.

Miscellaneous Expenses

DATE	PAYMENT TO	AMOUNT	REASON

Miscellaneous Expenses

Date	Payment To	Amount	Reason

Miscellaneous Expenses

DATE	PAYMENT TO	AMOUNT	REASON

MISCELLANEOUS EXPENSES

DATE	PAYMENT TO	AMOUNT	REASON

Miscellaneous Expenses

TAPE A 5" BY 7" MANILA ENVELOPE TO THIS PAGE TO KEEP YOUR RECEIPTS AND RECORDS FOR THIS CATEGORY ORGANIZED.

OFFICE EXPENSES

An author's main tool is a computer or laptop. After all, their life is writing. This means you need to keep track of these office expenses.

Do not confuse office expenses with office supplies, as the two categories are different.

Office supplies are a consumable product (there is a section in this book for that) that will have to be replenished, like paper, pens, etc.

Examples of office expenses include, but are not limited to:

– Computer - Laptop - iPad - Printer - Etc -

It is important to remember, a legitimate deduction requires the item to be a usual and reasonable expense for your line of work. So, for an author, a laptop will likely be viewed as a legitimate deduction.

However, if you use it for personal use, you will only be able to claim the percentage of time used for business.

EG: You buy a $500 laptop, and only use it 50% of the time for writing, then you're only able to claim a 50% usage.

OFFICE EXPENSES

DATE	PURCHASE LOCATION	AMOUNT	ITEMS

OFFICE EXPENSES

DATE	PURCHASE LOCATION	AMOUNT	ITEMS

OFFICE EXPENSES

TAPE A 5" BY 7" MANILA ENVELOPE TO THIS PAGE TO KEEP YOUR RECEIPTS AND RECORDS FOR THIS CATEGORY ORGANIZED.

OFFICE SUPPLIES

Authors go through a substantial amount of office supplies in the course of a year. Paper, printer ink, pens, note pads, folders, flash drives and more.

However, do not confuse office supplies with office expenses, as the two categories are different.

Office supplies are a consumable product that will have to be replenished, like paper, pens, etc.

Office expenses (there is a section in this book for that) include software (eg: Microsoft Word), internet costs, computers (under $2,500) etc.

Examples of office supplies include, but are not limited to:

– Printer Paper – Pens – Pencils – Printer Ink – Binder Clips –
– Flash Drives – Post-It Notes – Notebooks – Envelopes –

Note You are only allowed to deduct the cost of supplies used in the current year. For example, you find a great deal on printer paper and ink pens in December, you can't buy a huge quantity and consider it an expense in that year, since there's no way you could use it before the year ran out.

OFFICE SUPPLIES

DATE	PURCHASE LOCATION	AMOUNT	ITEMS

OFFICE SUPPLIES

DATE　　PURCHASE LOCATION　　　　AMOUNT　　　ITEMS

OFFICE SUPPLIES

DATE   PURCHASE LOCATION   AMOUNT   ITEMS

OFFICE SUPPLIES

DATE	PURCHASE LOCATION	AMOUNT	ITEMS

OFFICE SUPPLIES

TAPE A 5" BY 7" MANILA ENVELOPE TO THIS PAGE TO KEEP YOUR RECEIPTS AND RECORDS FOR THIS CATEGORY ORGANIZED.

PROFESSIONAL SERVICES

As a writer, you will most likely require the assistance of at least one, if not many, professionals. Editors, formatters, over designers, personal assistants, agents and more.

Being an author is anything but a solo career. It takes a team to get a book ready for publishing. And that team will cost money.

However, the benefit is, these costs are all tax deductible! Let's say you make $1,000 on a book, but you paid $300 for an editor, $200 for a cover and $100 for formatting. If you didn't deduct those costs, you would be stuck paying taxes on the entire $1,000. However, with those professional service deductions, ou would only be paying for taxes on $400 of that $1,000.

This is just one example of how important it is to keep track of these costs. Those deductions can add up to big savings come tax time.

PROFESSIONAL SERVICES

DATE	PAID TO	AMOUNT	REASON

PROFESSIONAL SERVICES

DATE	PAID TO	AMOUNT	REASON

PROFESSIONAL SERVICES

TAPE A 5" BY 7" MANILA ENVELOPE TO THIS PAGE TO KEEP YOUR RECEIPTS AND RECORDS FOR THIS CATEGORY ORGANIZED.

RESEARCH

For authors, research is an everyday part of the job. Many times it is a case of digging through the shelves at the library or searching all day on the internet. But sometimes, research requires special information.

Perhaps you need an unusual book on witchcraft to make your story believable. Not everyone knows everything about forensics, and crime scene television shows aren't a completely reliable source.

Other forms of research could include paying to shadow a certain individual in a special profession. Even the cost of visiting certain locations would be considered research *(though keep in mind the travel costs would go under travel, admission to a location like a haunted mine or other site would be the research).*

All the hard work you do to make your book better is important, and at least a portion of the cost is deductible!

RESEARCH

DATE	PAYMENT TO	AMOUNT	REASON

RESEARCH

DATE	PAYMENT TO	AMOUNT	REASON

RESEARCH

TAPE A 5" BY 7" MANILA ENVELOPE TO THIS PAGE TO KEEP YOUR RECEIPTS AND RECORDS FOR THIS CATEGORY ORGANIZED.

POSTAGE AND SHIPPING

In an internet driven world, some believe snail-mail is becoming obsolete. However, not for authors.

If you mail books to readers, manuscripts to agents or beta-readers, or even rent a PO box specifically for your writing (which is a good idea to prevent fans from getting your home address), these are deductible.

You can also deduct the cost of shipping your books to a location (like a book conference to avoid paying baggage claim at airport).

As long as what you're mailing or having shipped to you is business-related, you can deduct these costs.

Note The cost of envelopes, bubble wrap, packing tape, and other shipping supplies can be deducted, however those items are under office supplies, not shipping.

POSTAGE AND SHIPPING

DATE   PROVIDER (EG: USPS)   AMOUNT   REASON

POSTAGE AND SHIPPING

DATE   PROVIDER (EG: USPS)   AMOUNT   REASON

POSTAGE AND SHIPPING

DATE   PROVIDER (EG: USPS)   AMOUNT   REASON

POSTAGE AND SHIPPING

DATE   PROVIDER (EG: USPS)   AMOUNT   REASON

POSTAGE AND SHIPPING

TAPE A 5" BY 7" MANILA ENVELOPE TO THIS PAGE TO KEEP YOUR RECEIPTS AND RECORDS FOR THIS CATEGORY ORGANIZED.

TRAVEL

In general, authors tend to do a lot of traveling for their craft. Attending author conferences and book conventions all over the world can be costly, but also necessary to get your name out there. Thankfully, the travel expenses incurred on such trips are deductible on your taxes.

Some of the most common travel deductions are airline tickets, hotel, rental car, gas and cab fare. Additionally, any tolls and parking fees can be deducted. For these, simply keep your receipts and write what event it was for on it.

One of the trickier costs to deduct is if you drive your own vehicle during business travel. As an author, your car is nearly 100% used for personal use, therefore a depreciation deduction would not apply. However, you can deduct actual expenses (eg: fuel purchased during trip) or take the standard mileage rate. Generally, the actual expense is the simplest to deduct, as your receipts are readily available (however I have included some mileage pages in case you prefer the mileage method).

If you decide to bring your family along for the trip, only your expenses are deductible. That means any airline tickets, meals, etc. purchased for your children and/or spouse are not deductible.

Additionally, if you decide to extend your stay once the business is over, those additional days are not deductible. So if you purchase extra days at a hotel, extra days on a rental car, meals, etc; those additional expenses do not qualify.

Note Meals during travel are deductible but go in the 'Meals' category.

TRAVEL

DATE   PROVIDER (EG: DELTA, HERTZ)   AMOUNT   REASON

TRAVEL

DATE   PROVIDER (EG: DELTA, HERTZ)   AMOUNT   REASON

TRAVEL MILEAGE

DATE   STARTING ODOMETER/ENDING ODOMETER   REASON

TRAVEL MILEAGE

DATE   STARTING ODOMETER/ENDING ODOMETER   REASON

TRAVEL MILEAGE

DATE   STARTING ODOMETER/ENDING ODOMETER   REASON

TRAVEL MILEAGE

DATE   STARTING ODOMETER/ENDING ODOMETER   REASON

TRAVEL

TAPE A 5" BY 7" MANILA ENVELOPE TO THIS PAGE TO KEEP YOUR RECEIPTS AND RECORDS FOR THIS CATEGORY ORGANIZED.

www.ingramcontent.com/pod-product-compliance
Lightning Source LLC
Chambersburg PA
CBHW081635220526
45468CB00009B/2440